CHIPPING NORTON
RAILWAY

CHIPPING NORTON RAILWAY

ALAN WATKINS & BRENDA MORRIS

AMBERLEY

First published 2014

Amberley Publishing
The Hill, Stroud
Gloucestershire, GL5 4EP

www.amberley-books.com

978 1 4456 1884 5 (print)
978 1 4456 1863 0 (ebook)

British Library Cataloguing in Publication Data.
A catalogue record for this book is available from the British Library.

Typesetting by Amberley Publishing.
Printed in Great Britain.

CONTENTS

ACKNOWLEDGEMENTS

The photographs have been supplied courtesy of Alan Watkins, Brenda Morris and the Chipping Norton Museum of Local History. We would also like to thank Mrs Pauline Watkins and Miss Elizabeth Whitaker for their help.

FOREWORD

This book is not a definitive history of the branch line of the Great Western Railway (GWR) from Banbury to Cheltenham. It was never intended to be. Others have covered this in great detail. Instead, this book endeavours to show how the lives of those people who lived along the route from Chipping Norton to Kingham were enhanced by the coming of the railway. Today, there is no station at Chipping Norton, or the halt at Sarsden. There is scant evidence that a line existed. Chipping Norton has an antiques centre and a small industrial unit where once had been a bustling station yard; in fact, the sole building remaining from its earlier use is difficult to spot. It is situated behind the buildings of Cotteswood, the kitchen designers, next to the Royal Mail offices. Of Sarsden Halt, nothing remains. Only Kingham thrums to the sound of the Hereford–Worcester trains pulling in, before carrying their cargo of shoppers and commuters to Oxford and London Paddington. Cars fill the car park. Only the X8 bus traverses the route to and from Chipping Norton.

In the 1850s, the railway mattered; not just to industrialists and farmers seeking speedier ways of obtaining supplies and distributing goods, not just to people wanting to expand their markets, but to ordinary folk. It brought in newcomers, many of whom settled locally. It took local people away to new areas, if only for a day. There were accidents and tragedies, some of which are recorded here, but there was also a glamour about the gleaming engines huffing and puffing in the station. They sparked the imagination and raised aspirations.

This book has been compiled with the help of photographs, written accounts and stories by people to whom the railway means much, and to whom acknowledgement has been made elsewhere in the text. I am sure that we have not uncovered all that there is to tell, but we hope that you will enjoy reliving the tale of the Chipping Norton to Kingham Branch Railway, and that it will awaken stories of your own.

Liz Whitaker
2014

BRANCH TIMELINE

1846   First approaches to Oxford, Worcester & Wolverhampton Railway company (OW&WR) made by William Bliss.

1847   William Bliss writes second letter to OW&WR on 23 September.

1852   Third letter to OW&WR is written in April.

1853   Messrs Bliss and Wilkins and a deputation to OW&WR are again refused. Sir S. Morton, James Haughton Langston MP, and William Rollo decided to form a committee to start the Chipping Norton Railway.

1854   Work on the line starts in September with Peto & Betts as contractors, John Fowler as engineer, and 400 navvies.

1855   Line opens on 10 August.

1859   OW&WR purchase Chipping Norton Railway.

1861   West Midland Railway leased to Great Western Railway.

1862   Chipping Norton Junction (Kingham) to Bourton-on-the-Water line opens on 1 March.

1863   West Midland Railway merges with Chipping Norton branch line and comes under GWR control.

1884   New station built at Chipping Norton Junction.

1887   New Chipping Norton station opens on 2 April. A line from Chipping Norton to Banbury opens.

1906   Loop over main line opens at Chipping Norton Junction on 8 January with east and west signal boxes. Sarsden Halt is built.

1909   Chipping Norton Junction name changes to Kingham on 6 May.

1922   Kingham south signal box is closed and the north box name changes to Kingham station box on 4 November.

1951   Last passenger train from Chipping Norton to Banbury leaves on 2 January.

1953   The loop with the east and west signal boxes closes in September.

1962   Last passenger train from Chipping Norton to Kingham leaves on 3 December.

1966   Track from Chipping Norton to Kingham is lifted.

1970   Kingham station is rebuilt.

I.R

BOROUGH OF CHIPPING NORTON

Ja-Ja
REGD
TRADEMARK.

HERALDIC SERIES.

1

KINGHAM TO
CHIPPING NORTON RAILWAY

At a time when there are disputes about the desirability of constructing a high-speed railway across beautiful countryside, it is interesting to note that the reasons for so doing are similar to those that promoted the Oxford, Worcester & Wolverhampton Railway (OW&WR) and one of its feeder lines – the rural branch line of the Chipping Norton Railway. This company was formed in 1853 with the object of connecting the OW&WR main line to Chipping Norton, 4½ miles east.

The OW&WR was built to standard gauge. It had been promoted by the industrialists of the Midlands, anxious to deliver their goods and coal more speedily to more markets. The line at Chipping Norton was built to the standard gauge of 4 feet 8½ inches and was therefore compatible with that of the OW&WR.

It was a desire for increased trade and markets that led to the development of the main line railway system. So it was with Chipping Norton. The idea of a branch line of the OW&WR fitted in with the desires of two leading traders from Chipping Norton. William Bliss had inherited his father's highly successful tweed mill. It was powered by steam and the coal was brought in from Banbury. Before the railway, the empty horse-drawn wagons would be taken from Chipping Norton to Chapel House toll gate at midnight, a toll ticket would be bought and they would travel on to Banbury. They would load up with coal and return within twenty-four hours to avoid a second toll fee and cut costs a little. William Bliss needed a regular supply of 3,500 tons of coal a year to power his upper mill. He was, therefore, in the light of previous difficulties, an enthusiast for the railway.

William S. Hitchman, the owner of a brewery in the town, also had an interest in a more efficient way of obtaining coal, as well as a way of distributing his beer further. So, the line eventually came: 4½ miles long (or, more accurately, 4 miles and 42 chains long), linking Sarsden, Churchill and Kingham. It was paid for by Sir Samuel Morton Peto, a major investor and an important contractor with a vested interest. One should never forget that however beneficial a project turns out to be, it originates in the minds of those who benefit most, at least in the early stages. William Bliss and William Hitchman were major investors and others followed. The overall director was John Fowler.

Chipping Norton station looking from Mill Road.

Building for the Kingham to Chipping Norton branch line started in September 1854, and it was opened on 10 August 1855. At the time, it was the first privately built community railway line.

There was a considerable amount of correspondence and general discussion before any suggestions were seriously considered. Below are extracts from the minute book of the OW&WR.

20 August 1845	A memorial received through A. L. Rowlinson, signed by the mayor of Chipping Norton on behalf of the council was read.
26 January 1847	A memorial from the inhabitants of Chipping Norton and neighbourhood recommending a branch line to that town.
5 October 1847	A letter from Mr William Bliss to Mr W. Lewis, secretary of the Oxford Worcester & Wolverhampton Railway Company.

William Bliss wrote personally to the OW&WR to persuade them of the advantage of a branch line to Chipping Norton. Receiving no positive response from them in 1846, he wrote again on 23 September 1847.

Below is the letter recorded in the minute book of the OW&WR, which was read out at their meeting on 5 October 1847:

Dear Sir,

On my return today I hoped to have found a line or two from you informing me what decision (if any) was come to at your meeting last Tuesday respecting the result of the survey which you made of this part of the line last Monday week.

I now trouble you with this to enquire how we had better proceed to bring the matter fairly before your Board – it appears to me that as we have already addressed two Memorials (signed by very respectable inhabitants of this Town and neighbourhood) as well as letter to your Chairman and a letter to Mr Brunel – it now only remains for us to appoint a deputation to wait upon and press our interest upon your notice and I shall be glad if you will let me know what will be the best way and fittest time to do so.

We are determined if possible to have Railway communication with the Town and if you are not willing to give it us the sooner we know it the better as we shall then at once proceed to open a negotiation with the London and North Western Interest at Banbury who have already made some overtures to us.

Seeing that Chipping Norton is the most important place you will have on your line between Evesham and Oxford (a distance of 36 to 38 miles) our tonnage being about 3,500 tons annually, I cannot think that you will consult your own Interest by letting this Town and Neighbourhood fall into the hands of your opponents which it most certainly will if you do not give us a Passenger's Station at Bledington Mill. A Station at Adlestrop Gate and Shipton Bridge will be of little or no service to us and instead of leaving our interest in the hands of Local Directors I wish you and a few others of the Directors would visit this Town and see what interest we have to offer, or if you can make an appointment with your Chairman to receive a deputation we shall be glad to wait upon you at any place or at any time.

Waiting the favour of a reply to this, I am, Dear Sir,

Yours truly,

W. Bliss

P.S. You must bear in mind that we are the connecting line between your line and Banbury and that there is only seventeen miles of rail wanted to connect the Wash with the Bristol Channel or the East and West Coast of this Island which I think may ultimately be of great importance.

The company took the letter seriously because they had to. They discussed it and, as we can see, transcribed it into their minute book. However, they were not convinced by the arguments.

From the tone of this letter, we can see how determined William Bliss was to have a branch line to Chipping Norton. He was even willing to threaten to open negotiations with a rival company – the London & North Western Railway – in order to awaken the interest of the OW&WR in Chipping Norton. He mentions the futility as far as he is concerned of stations at Shipton Bridge and Adlestrop. It is amusing to note that five months later the company received a request from Lord Leigh of Adlestrop House. He wanted a signal stop for first-class trains to stop at Adlestrop station in order that passengers for Adlestrop House could be taken up and put down. Such were the desires of prominent men.

In April 1852, because the OW&WR had almost completed their line from Worcester to Evesham, Chipping Norton again approached the company with a third request for a line, persisting in their efforts to be connected to the OW&WR. In 1853, the OW&WR had completed their own line linking Oxford with the West Midland towns, so there was therefore more incentive to make a connection.

William Bliss began to install machinery to change the mill to steam by buying an engine to power his looms and carding room. Other local business people supported him, one of these being William Simkins Hitchman of Hitchman Breweries.

These two gentlemen became the two main figures in support of a connecting branch line to Chipping Norton. In 1851, there had been a report of a public meeting in Banbury promoting the building of a line to connect Banbury to the OW&WR line with Moreton-in-Marsh, the main promoters being the farmers of the Stour Valley. They wanted to transport their produce quickly and cheaply to the market in Banbury. William Bliss and William Hitchman were dismayed at this suggestion, as Chipping Norton would have been completely isolated if the OW&WR again refused their request. The two gentlemen then approached James Houghton Langston MP, who resided at the nearby Sarsden House, as they wanted support from an influential party. This was particularly important as most of the land required for the building of the branch line belonged to James Langston. They also approached Samuel Morton Peto, who was a major supporter of the

William Bliss.

OW&WR. He agreed that the OW&WR would work the proposed branch line as an integral part of their own system. Samuel Morton Peto also became a major investor in the Chipping Norton Railway and therefore had considerable influence over the entire project. He had worked for his uncle's contracting company and, in 1830, had inherited half of the firm in conjunction with his cousin, Thomas Grissell. By 1840, Peto had already constructed many railways in partnership with Edward Ladd Betts, and had secured major interests in companies like the Eastern Counties, East Suffolk and Oxford, Worcester & Wolverhampton Railways.

After many meetings, William Bliss, William Hitchman and Sir Morton Peto decided to finance the building of the branch line to Chipping Norton. A Bill was sought in the House of Commons that granted permission for the construction of the line 'to be situated midway between Shipton and Adlestrop stations, where a house has to be erected for the sale of tickets' and terminating in Chipping Norton. The proposed line would be 4 miles 42 chains long, and the sum of £26,000 was authorised to be raised. Sir Morton Peto provided £14,000, while the remaining £12,000 was subscribed by William Bliss, William Hitchman and other local investors.

A route was chosen that ran north-east from Chipping Norton Junction to the terminus at Chipping Norton, following the valley of the River Swale. Construction began in August 1854 directed by John Fowler, who had replaced Isambard Kingdom Brunel as chief engineer of the OW&WR. As this was Sir Morton Peto's own firm, they obviously had the contract.

The railway was completed in around nine months, but problems arose when the Board of Trade inspector objected to a level crossing that had been completed near the village of Cornwell. Level crossings were seen as a source of danger, particularly during the early days of railway construction. This level crossing was

Sir Samuel Morton Peto.

about 1½ miles to the south of Chipping Norton, and carried a minor road across the railway; this route was used as a shortcut between Chipping Norton and the OW&WR station at Adlestrop. The inspector was informed that this traffic would cease when the line was open, as goods and passengers would travel to and from the new station at Chipping Norton. The railway line would be opened for goods traffic first, and passengers would be allowed to travel it a few months later.

Most of the materials for the laying of the track were brought down the OW&WR line and were held at Kingham until the track began to be laid for the new line. The final building was completed in August 1855 and a huge celebration dinner was held in Chipping Norton Town Hall at 3 p.m. on 10 August.

The extract from the *Banbury Guardian* describes the opening celebrations:

OPENING OF THE BRANCH RAILWAY

At length, after long demur and frequent postponement, we are able, on good authority to announce that this line will be opened in about 10 days. On Thursday morning the engineer and several gentlemen connected with the line, came by special train, and the result of their visit is that the bridge, about which so much has been said, will be built under a guarantee, for which the Board of Trade will permit the line to be opened.

Cornwell Road Bridge today.

The following is an extract from the August 1855 edition of the *Oxford Chronicle and Berks and Bucks Gazette*:

The formal opening of the Chipping Norton branch of the Oxford, Worcester and Wolverhampton Railway took place on Friday, the 10th, and the event was celebrated by the inhabitants of the locality in a manner which shows how highly they appreciated the importance of the railway and the benefits it was calculated to confer upon the district generally. The railway was 4½ miles in length, and consisted of a single line of rails, the gradients throughout being easy. It commenced at a junction with the main line situated in the parish of Churchill, about three quarters of a mile below the Shipton station. The question of forming a line of railway to this small town had been considered for several years but little progress had been made towards a practical realisation of the wishes of the inhabitants until the Mayor of Chipping Norton took the matter in hand. The Parliamentary Act was obtained, and in August of the year 1854, the work was begun by the firm of Peto and Betts.

The Board of Trade eventually gave the company permission to open the railway for general traffic, on the Company giving a guarantee to erect bridges when required to do so. The Oxford, Worcester and Wolverhampton Company undertook to work the line, taking 50 per cent of the revenue, the remainder being paid as dividend to the shareholders, so that of every shilling the Company took the shareholders received sixpence. The Company also agreed to keep the line in thorough repair, to purchase the plant and working materials, and to pay to the Chipping Norton shareholders a fair proportion of the profits brought by means of the branch to the main line. A clause was inserted in the act enabling the Oxford, Worcester and Wolverhampton Company to purchase the shares at par, paying fair interest to the shareholders for their capital, so 'there is a great probability that in a few years hence the borough will enjoy the immense advantages of a direct railway communication to London and the north-west without incurring any of the risk arising from the fluctuations which occasionally deteriorate railway investments.'

Shortly after twelve o'clock on Friday, Sir S. M. Peto, Bart., accompanied by Lady Peto, Miss Peto, Mrs Kemp, Miss Broadbent, Noel T. Smith Esq., (Secretary of the Oxford, Worcester and Wolverhampton Railway), John Parson Esq., (Deputy Chairman of the Oxford, Worcester and Wolverhampton Railway), John Fowler Esq. (Chief Engineer of the line) and Mr Johnson Esq., a Director of the Company, arrived by special train at the Chipping Norton Junction. The band played 'See the Conquering Hero Comes'. They were met at the station by William Bliss Esq., Mayor of Chipping Norton, Alderman Lewis (of Worcester) and G. H. Busby Esq., also Directors of the Company. Also attending were Messrs Rawlinson, Weston, Aplin, Tilsley, Wilkins, who were professional men of the town. Mr Lockey the Surveyor, Members of the Committee: T. Rolls, R. Guy, T. Keck, J. Loveland, T. Hopgood, J. H. Kingdom, J. Ward. A considerable number of respectable inhabitants of the locality were congregated at the station, which was decorated with evergreens and banners, besides other indications of pleasure appropriate to the occasion. A few yards from the platform was erected a triumphal arch, in evergreens and flowers, surmounted with the arms of England, France and Turkey, indicative of the firm alliance that now subsists between these countries. The Directors, with great consideration and kindness, issued 500 free tickets to enable the inmates and children at the workhouse, and the poorer classes generally, to enjoy a trip to and from the Junction. A small locomotive, named *Eugenie* in honour of the French Empress, and gaily decorated with banners, conveyed the train to Chipping Norton, where it arrived shortly before one o'clock amid the cheers of a large assemblage of the inhabitants. The station house and its vicinity presented a very cheerful and animated appearance.

The feeling of the whole town was of a very enthusiastic character. All the shops were closed; flags were flying from various parts of the borough; the church bells rang a peal; a brass band from Blockley played an inspiring march during the day. As a contemporary report stated 'the example set by this "independent" little place is one that not only does it infinite credit, but will we trust be followed by hundreds of towns situated within short distances from through lines of railway'.

On leaving the station, the visitors proceeded to the Mayor's residence where a party numbering between twenty and thirty partook of an elegant luncheon. On the conclusion of the banquet the following ladies honoured the meeting with their presence. Lady Peto, Miss Peto, Mrs Kemp, Miss Broadbent, the Mayoress and the Misses Bliss, Mrs Wishaw, Mrs Rawlinson and Miss Rawlinson, Mrs G. Tilsley, Miss Kemble, Mrs Hitchman and Miss Hitchman, Mrs H. Tilsley, Mrs Kingdom, Mrs Southam, Mrs Huckvale, Mrs Youngman, Mrs W. Biggerstaff, Mrs T. Biggerstaff and others. A very handsome silver salver and a cake basket at a cost of 70 guineas was handed over as a testimony to the Mayor. Afterwards they all proceeded to Mr Bliss's new factory. This was in the process of being erected near the railway station, where about two hundred and fifty men, women and children in his employ were provided by him with a substantial dinner, furnished by Mrs Bishop of the Crown and Cushion Inn. The health of Sir S. M. Peto and Lady Peto were drunk in an enthusiastic manner, and the former responded to the compliment with an appropriate address. He had been told that the source operatives of Chipping Norton presented a striking and favourable contrast to the factory operatives in the north of England, and that, as regarded healthiness of appearance and general character they could not be surpassed. 'He was glad to see such a kind feeling appeared to exist between them and their employer, which was creditable to both parties, and he [Sir S. M. Peto] would be rejoiced; to see a similar feeling universally extended.' He then congratulated them on the opening of a railway line into their town and expressed a hope and confident belief that all classes, from the highest to the lowest, would benefit by it. The baronet was apparently heartily cheered on the conclusion of his address. Several other toasts were proposed and on leaving, the Mayor expressed a hope that they would enjoy themselves during the afternoon, and complimented them upon the manner in which they had conducted themselves, which was equally creditable to them as it was gratifying to him. The visitors were loudly cheered on leaving the factory.

The public dinner to celebrate this auspicious event took place at three o'clock in the Town Hall, which was neatly decorated for the occasion. A banner bearing the inscription 'Unrestricted Commerce, the people's friend' was placed at the head of the room, and another was at the bottom with 'Extension of Education'. In other parts of the room were a number of banners belonging to the Cordwainers Company, Oxford, which were loaned for the purpose. The dinner was provided by Mr Parker (late Beck) of the White Hart Hotel, whose efforts on the occasion were highly commended. The dinner was sumptuous and the wines, port, sherry and champagne considered exceptional. The menu was as follows:

Fish Course – Salmon, filleted soles, stewed eels.

First Course – Quarters of lamb; dishes of roast beef; shoulders of lamb; loins of veal; hams; dishes of chicken and tongue; pigeon pies; dishes of cutlets; dishes of sweetbreads; vol-au-vents; dishes of curried rabbit; dishes of hashed calves head; green geese; couples of ducks.

Second Course – Cabinet and plum puddings; noyau and wine jellies; creams; trifles; dishes of pastry; tarts; chicken and lobster salads.

Desserts – Dishes of grapes; melons; pineapples; dishes of gooseberries; dishes of plums; dishes of French plums; dishes of almonds and raisins; dishes of biscuits; dishes of currents; raspberries; apples and cherries.

Some excellent wines, including a bountiful supply of champagne, accompanied the dinner, and added greatly to the enjoyment of the guests, who numbered about 120.

At the dinner, Mr Langston was applauded for his interest, efforts and assistance. His steward replied on behalf of Mr Langston, who was not at Sarsden House at the time as he had had an accident. Mr Langston had written a letter hoping that the railway would help Chipping Norton to maintain its present and past position, and that it would be a means of increased prosperity to the town.

The hospitalities were not limited to the Town Hall and to those who assembled there. On the Common a fair was held, where there were booths for entertainments, swings and stalls for the juveniles and a fat sheep roasted for those who desired to partake of it. Cricket matches were played so that there was something for everyone to enjoy. The masons and carpenters employed by Mr Bliss, in number about 50, were given by Mr Bliss an excellent dinner at the Unicorn Inn. The railway porters were similarly treated at the Blue Boar Inn; the band and constables at the Fox Inn; and the ringers at Kightley's Railway Hotel in the New Street.

The station consisted of a single platform and a two-storey building. There are no photographs in existence, but the Bliss tweed mill shows a drawing of the station on their publicity stationery. There was also a water tank, a single-road engine shed and a goods shed provided. A wooden roof was later added following complaints by passengers who were exposed to the elements while waiting on the platform. The gasworks, originally in Distons Lane in the town, were relocated adjacent to the Tweed Mill in 1872, and a new siding was provided for this purpose.

In 1860, the OW&WR amalgamated with two other railway companies to form the West Midland Railway. When the West Midland Railway amalgamated with the GWR in 1863, Chipping Norton became part of the Great Western system.

When the Chipping Norton line eventually progressed towards Banbury, the old station was no longer required and was duly demolished. A new goods yard was

Public Dinner at the Town Hall
to Commemorate the opening of the
Chipping Norton Branch Railway

Menu
Quarters of Lamb – Shoulders of Lamb
Dishes of Roast Beef
Loins of Veal – Hams
Dishes of chicken and tongue
Dishes of cutlets
Dishes of sweetbreads Dishes of hashed calves head
Pigeon Pies
Vol-au-vents
Dishes of curried rabbit – Green geese
Couples of ducks
..........o..........
Cabinet Puddings – plum puddings
Noyeau jellies – wine jellies
Creams – trifles
Dishes of pastry – tarts
Chicken salads – Lobster salads
..........o..........
Dishes of grapes, melons, pineapples, gooseberries
Dishes of plums, French plums, almonds and raisins
Dishes of biscuits, currants, raspberries, apples and cherries

The menu for the public dinner, held to celebrate the opening of the Chipping Norton branch.

erected on the old station building site. In 1922, the engine shed was closed and has been demolished by 1947.

When the new station was built, it was sited on a curve as it was on the Down side. A very small shelter was built on the Up side. A very fine lattice girder footbridge linked the two platforms. Two signal boxes were needed: Chipping Norton East on the station platform, and Chipping Norton West near to the Bliss Tweed Mill. In August 1929, the west box was demolished and the east box was renamed Chipping Norton signal box.

In 1904, a stable block was built to house the railway's horses. It was no longer required after 1921 as the railway contracted out delivery work, and was then used to house the GWR buses. The stable is now the only building surviving at the Chipping Norton station.

The first engines or locomotives were used to work the line were Nos 52 and 53. No. 52 was called *Ben Johnson* and No. 53 was known as *Mrs Johnson*. They had American-style cabs and were small. They were retired in 1877.

The railway was of enormous benefit to Messrs Hitchman and Bliss in particular, whose products found more distant markets more quickly. We have noted how farmers, too, used the railway to transport cattle, milk and other products, but what about the ordinary inhabitants of Chipping Norton? What did they gain? Right from the beginning, coal was important. Not only did it provide the power for the local industries, but also for home fires, and was cheaper than coal brought from the canal at Banbury.

In 1863, a co-operative movement started – the Chipping Norton Co-operative Coal Society. It advertised 'A WHARF' at the railway station for good and cheap coals. The bold capital letters of the announcement signalled the importance of the venture. 'Cobbles' were sold at 15s per ton, and 'Best Coal' at 16s 6d. The coal was delivered in Chipping Norton at 1s 6d per ton extra, all to be paid for in cash only. There was no question of owing for your coal or for 'putting it on the slate'. The secretary of the society was Mr E. Bishop, who lived in New Street. If you bought your coal directly from the wharf, you bought it from Mr J. Belcher, who was described as the society's servant. Later, other coal merchants sold their wares from the station ground – Mr E. Stanley and Mr E. F. W. Johnson for example.

One can imagine the changes in the houses when coal replaced wood as fuel. No longer did they have the sweet smell of applewood or the bright, cheerful flames of beech logs; dark coal awaited the bellows in the grate instead. The outside air would eventually become sootier, leaving dark streaks on the house walls.

In the station grounds were the Chipping Norton Gasworks. The original gasworks were situated in Distons Lane where houses – Nos 37, 39 and 41 – now stand. Mr William Morley Stears, a gas engineer from Stroud, was the man largely responsible for the introduction of gas to Chipping Norton. At a special meeting of the council held in the town hall on 26 July 1836, he submitted his proposal to light the public lamps in the town with gas, and to supply private houses, shops and other businesses. The proposal being passed, he purchased a cottage and garden in Distons Lane for £150 to erect the gasworks. A company called the Chipping

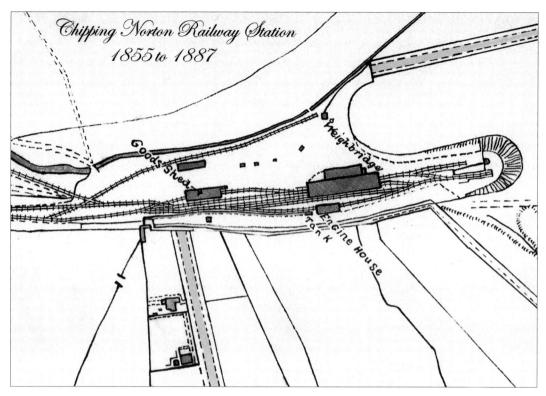

The station yard post-1887.

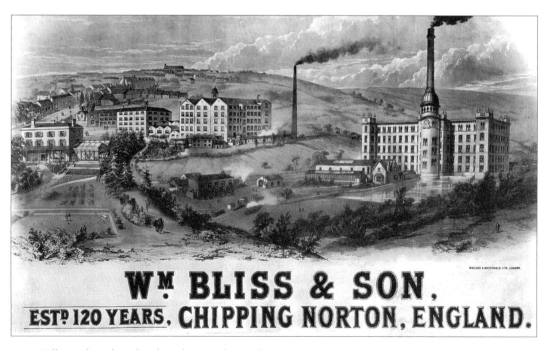

William Bliss's letterheading showing both of his mills and the railway.

A drawing of the original station.

The new station shortly after it was built, *c.* 1890.

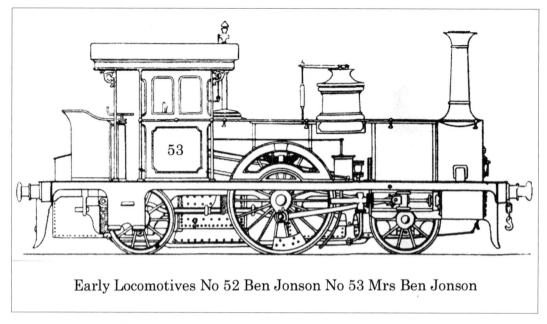

Early Locomotives No 52 Ben Jonson No 53 Mrs Ben Jonson

An early engine (No. 53) as used on the line.

Thomas Edward Stanley's coal yard on the station site.

The Co-operative's coal wharf. From left to right, back row: Mr Latham, Jesse Hadlan, Tom Hill. Front row: Alf Doman, foreman Charlie Winnet and Jack Bolter.

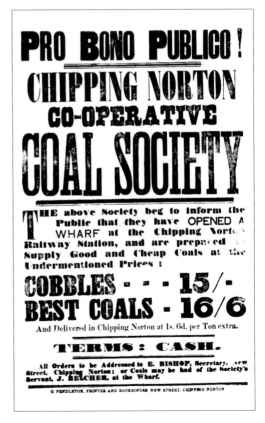

A handbill advertising Co-operative coal.

Norton Gas & Coke Company was formed and issued shares at £10 each. For the sum of £1,696 19s, he promised to allow for twelve street lamps to be erected, but it was later decided to erect twenty-eight street lamps. An agreement was made with the Corporation of Chipping Norton to light each lamp from August to April within one hour after sunset until two hours before sunrise at a cost of £3 per lamp per year. A fine of 6d per night was to be forfeited for each lamp neglected to be so lit.

The gasworks were completed in 1837, and Mr Whitaker was appointed 'Conductor of Works' for 17s per week. John Matthews was the assistant and Richard Padley was later employed. Gas, being lighter than air, rises, and for this reason the works were sited at the lowest part of town.

Mr William Bliss, having built his new factory in the valley in 1855 wished to use gas and it became necessary to move the gasworks. A site was therefore purchased below the new mill around 1857. When the rail came, the gasworks were conveniently placed alongside.

More employment came with the railway. Instead of the seasonal work of the farm labourer with its capricious wage, there was the opportunity of a regular wage for regular work, and a chance of promotion. Staff was needed for the station, the goods and the locomotives. There was also the chance of working away from the town. But most of all were the opportunities the railway afforded for fun. You could travel at a reasonable rate for a day out – Barry Island was a popular destination, as was Weymouth. For a day by the sea you left Chipping Norton at 3.30 a.m., arriving at Weymouth at 9 a.m. Stretching before you was a day of glorious freedom until you set off home on the 10 p.m. train to arrive in Chipping Norton at 3.30 a.m. One wonders how they filled twelve hours if the weather turned wet.

It is amazing to think that in 1902 one could catch a train in Chipping Norton on a Monday or Tuesday to holiday in Guernsey or Jersey in the Channel Islands. If only one could that now. One such excursion was arranged by the Chipping Norton Deanery in 1886. Residents from the parishes of Chadlington, Charlbury, Chipping Norton, Enstone, Fifield, Heythrop, Leafield, Little Tew and Milton-under-Wychwood were invited to attend. The *Chipping Norton Deanery Magazine* 1886 quotes the following:

EXCURSION TO THE SEASIDE
This excursion to Southampton has been approved and is for the Church Workers, for several parishes, although others in the Deanery will be welcome to join, so far as it is possible without exceeding the limit of 400. Please send in your names as soon as possible to your local Clergy, together with 5/6d being the cost of the railway fare. Residents in other parishes are welcome for the extra cost of 1/-. The excursion will take place on Tuesday 8th June. The remaining 5/- (for breakfast, dinner, tea and steamer) will be payable on or before 1st June. After arriving at Southampton, breakfast with cold meat will be provided and then we will embark on the steamer and take a trip to Portsmouth and the Isle of Wight. Dinner (beer extra) will be served on board. Tea will be served in Southampton before returning home

Above and below: Chipping Norton Gasworks showing the private line alongside the station.

Mr Harry Beale working at the gasworks.

Chipping Norton Gas & Coke Co.
erecting a new gas holder.

A bride and groom leaving for their honeymoon by train.

JUNE 20 1883

THE OXFORDSHIRE WEEKLY NEWS, WEDNESD

GREAT WESTERN RAILWAY (WEST MID SECTION.)

The GWR timetable for June 1883.

1902
GREAT WESTERN RAILWAY.

EXCURSIONS will run as under:—

TUESDAY, JULY 15.—DAY TRIP to BIRMINGHAM and WOLVERHAMPTON (Exhibition), from Bourton-on-Water, Chipping Norton, Adderbury, etc.

WEDNESDAY MORNING, JULY 16.—To PORTSMOUTH (Exhibition) and BOURNEMOUTH, for 1, 3, 6, 10 or 13 days, from Evesham, Shipston-on-Stour, Moreton-in-Marsh, Andoversford, Bourton-on-Water, Chipping Norton, Charlbury, etc.

SUNDAY NIGHT, JULY 21.—To BRISTOL, Taunton, Exeter, Dawlish, Teignmouth, Torquay and Plymouth, for 1 or 11 days, from Evesham, Moreton-in-Marsh, Chipping Norton, Charlbury, etc.

Until further notice, EXCURSIONS will run as under:—

EVERY MONDAY.—To Guernsey and Jersey, for a fortnight or less, from Evesham, Moreton-in-Marsh, Chipping Norton, Charlbury and Witney.

EVERY MONDAY and FRIDAY (except August 1 and 4).—To Winchester, Gosport, Bournemouth, Portsmouth, Southampton, Ryde and Cowes, for a week, a fortnight, etc., from Evesham, Moreton-in-Marsh, Chipping Norton, Charlbury, Witney and Eynsham.

EVERY FRIDAY.—To Yeovil, Dorchester and Weymouth, for 8 or 15 days, from Evesham, Moreton-in-Marsh, Chipping Norton, Charlbury, Witney and Eynsham. To Brighton, Hastings, Canterbury, Dover, Eastbourne, Ramsgate, Margate, etc., for 8 or 15 days, from Evesham, Moreton-in-Marsh and Chipping Norton.

For Times, Bookings from other Stations, WEEK-END EXCURSIONS, Country Lodgings, etc., see Bills and Pamphlets.

J. L. WILKINSON,
General Manager.

The list of excursions available from Chipping Norton station.

The Channel Island of Jersey.

EXCURSION TO SOUTHAMPTON

The following times have been fixed by the GWR for the train to leave the respective stations, Chipping Norton 4.50 a.m.; Chipping Norton Junction 5.10 a.m.; Shipton 5.15 a.m.; Acott 5.20 a.m.; Charlbury 5.30 a.m. The train will arrive at Southampton at 8.32 a.m. and will leave on the return journey at 7 p.m. Dinner, consisting of a hot meal, two vegetables, bread and either a bottle of lemonade or a cup of coffee will be probably provided at Miss Robinson's 'Sailors' Welcome' close to the harbour at Portsmouth. It may be interesting to some of our readers to know that Miss Robinson is generally known as 'the soldier's and sailor's friend', owing to the great and kind work that she had done among them, by means of the Sailors' Welcome, and other institutions she has established. Formerly when these defenders of their country arrived at Portsmouth they were turned out of their ship, with nowhere to go to, except to the lowest public houses, where their wages were soon wasted with nothing to show for them, except bad habits contracted. They were shunned by every respectable person. Miss Robinson has changed all that, and many interesting and touching stories are told of how she has been the means of saving many a poor fellow, who, having escaped the fury and waves of the sea, was rapidly being drowned in the deep flood of temptation which awaited him as soon as he put his foot on dry ground. The interest attached to these houses of welcome is increased when it is remembered that Miss Robinson is a confirmed invalid, and has now, for some years, been completely bed-ridden.

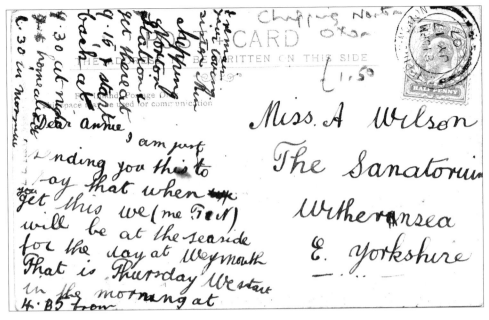

A postcard with details describing a day trip starting from Chipping Norton station.

Many trains packed with day trippers left Chipping Norton station over the years.

The Packer family were especially fond of rail travel and were known to go out for the day on a regular basis. As Mr Frank Packer was a well-known photographer, there are some lovely photographs showing the family enjoying themselves on the local railway.

Animals, too, used the railway. The Heythrop Hunt hounds were kennelled by the railway, just off Worcester Road in Chipping Norton, and the hounds were often exercised in the adjacent fields. Sometimes they and the horses were transported by rail to meets several miles away – for example, near Bourton-on-the-Water and Notgrove.

The inauguration of the luncheon corridor express service between Cardiff and Newcastle, with connections at Banbury, was a great success; the train, both on the Up and Down journeys, being well patronised by long-distance passengers. It was the longest cross-country service in England at the time, being 145 miles in extent, and passed through seven counties. The service was made possible by an arrangement between the GWR, the GCR and NER. The journey took 8½ hours and was of great benefit to the commercial centres. From Cardiff the route went to Newport, with easy connections from Aberdare, Merthyr, Hereford and Pontypool, and skirted the River Wye to Gloucester and Cheltenham. From Cheltenham it proceeded through Chipping Norton Junction to Banbury, then on to Rugby, Leicester, Nottingham and Sheffield. It was possible to stop the train at any station in between if notice was given to the driver beforehand. Many passengers alighted at Chipping Norton station.

Nationally, three circuses are known to have moved their animals by train. Bertram Mills moved elephants and horses, and Billy Smart used the railways to move everything. However, when Chipperfield's Circus purchased the old sawmill at Heythrop in the 1950s, they made it their winter quarters and training ground. It was very cold the first winter there and the Heythrop farm had little protection from the weather. Their large troop of eight elephants arrived at Chipping Norton by train. Led by elephants Leila and Mary, with trainer Peter Larrigan and young Dickie Chipperfield, they proceeded through the town on their way to their winter quarters at Heythrop. Many of the inhabitants of Chipping Norton turned out to gaze at Chipperfield's impressive line of elephants disembarking from the train and swaying away gracefully through the town, trunk to tail. You could say that it gave 'trunk line' a whole new meaning.

Another exciting event for the town, only much earlier, was the arrival of an aeroplane at the station. Gustav Hamel, of Eton and Cambridge, was an aviation pioneer. On 9 September 1911, he flew the world's first scheduled airmail service – the Coronation Aerial Post from Hendon to Windsor. In February 1913, to much excitement in Chipping Norton, he brought his Blériot Mark II aircraft (with no ailerons) by train and then assembled it for a flying display on the brewery field (now Chipping Norton School playing field). Gustav Hamel died in a flying accident the following year while crossing the Channel.

At the start of the First World War, the line was used to transport soldiers who volunteered their services to their country. The following photographs show how many answered their country's call to serve.

Mrs Frank Packer and son Basil with grandma, Mrs Todd, going on a journey.

The Heythrop hunt hounds exercising by the railway lines.

Chipperfield's elephants walking down Station Approach at the start of a journey by train.

Getting ready to be loaded on to the train.

The elephants being loaded on to the train.

Waiting to go into the carriages.

Elephants loaded and ready to be off.

The elephants walking through Chipping Norton after arriving by train. The lead elephants are Leila and Mary, with trainer Peter Larrigan.

After the invasion of Belgium in the First World War, nearly a quarter of a million Belgians fled to England in 1914. Some of these Belgian refugees arrived at Chipping Norton station, having been invited to the town by the borough council. The Manor House was set aside for them, while Miss Doris Mace collected for their maintenance. Groups of people from the town made themselves responsible for individual families. The Chipping Norton Co-operative Society allowed one family to live in No. 2 High Street and supplied their needs. Many years later, while on holiday in Belgium, Mr Reg Johnson – the well-known saddler in the town – renewed his acquaintance with one family who still had pleasant memories of their stay in Chipping Norton.

There were unusual uses made of the railway area, however. Fred Scarsbrook, the owner of a grocery shop in New Street, kept chickens on railway land near the tunnel that was built later to take the trains on to Banbury. He used to go down to the railway embankment to feed them twice a day, locking them in their coop in the evenings to save them from foxes. Records do not show if they laid well. Today, the entrance to the tunnel is bricked up and locked to deter visitors, as it is now a designated bat sanctuary.

On 1 September 1939, children who attended the New City Road School in Plaistow attended school as usual. The only difference on that day was that each child was carrying a new gas mask in a brown cardboard box with string attached

The aeroplane of Gustav Hamel being unloaded from the train at Chipping Norton.

Mr Hamel and plane ready for transportation to the field with porter Fred Morse.

The Mark II aircraft ready to fly.

The flying display.

Troops waiting on the platform at Chipping Norton station after manoeuvres.

Oxford University Officer Training Corps at Chipping Norton on one of their exercises.

O.U.O.T.C. FIELD OPERATIONS, 13 - LOADING THE GUNS - CHIPPINGNORTON STATION -

Oxford University Officer Trainer Corps loading guns.

ENGLAND DECLAR
SER^T BAKER AND THREE VOLUNTEER'S F   SERVICE 1914 N°1

Sergeant Baker and three volunteers preparing to leave for war, 1914.

E Company 4th Battalion on their way to the station, 1914.

Soldiers going to war on the train to Southampton.

St John's Ambulance men going off to active service.

National Reserve Service Section on parade at the station.

Above, below and next page: Belgian refugees arriving at Chipping Norton station in 1914.

CHIPPING NORTON WELCOMES SOME BELGIAN REFUGEE'S 1914 N°6

CHIPPING NORTON WELCOMES SOME BELGIAN REFUGEE'S 1914 N°4

to carry it over the shoulder, a small bag with a change of clothes and a packed lunch. Each child was also given a stick of barley sugar in case they felt sick on the train. Needless to say, there was hardly any barley sugar left by the time the train arrived at Chipping Norton station. It was said to be the longest train to arrive at the station. Local children were amazed as they looked down from the road bridge to see the numbers of children arriving. The London children then walked up the hill in New Street to the New Cinema where they were given drinks and something to eat. Local families were waiting for them and the children were then introduced to their adoptive families, authorities tried to insist that brothers and sisters were to be kept together. The teachers from New City Road School also came with their children and from then onwards, the evacuees were given school lessons in the mornings and the Chipping Norton children had their lessons in the

Mr Fred Scarsbrook kept a chicken run beside the line.

Left: The tunnel by the station is now closed and locked as it is a bat sanctuary.

Below: Children playing on the bridge beside the tunnel.

103.

THE LEYS. CHIPPING NORTON
FROM THE TUNNEL

Mrs Grace Packer sitting on the abutment to the road bridge with a clear view down the path to the station.

The abutment where Mrs Packer is sitting in the previous photograph as it is today.

Chipping Norton station in August 1958, note there are no awnings.

The capping bricks on the bridge showing alterations that have been carried out soon after the completion in 1896.

afternoons. After several weeks, some of the children were homesick and returned to their families in London, but quite a few stayed until the end of hostilities. If any of the London children had attended a grammar school before the war, they automatically attended the Chipping Norton County Grammar School in Burford Road. Eventually, the evacuees were amalgamated with the Chipping Norton children and they all attended school together.

The following day saw another large train pull into the station. This time it had mothers, babies and young children on board. Many of these were accommodated in the local villages.

The year 1907 saw a crash (reported as a smash) at Chipping Norton. It was described as a peculiar incident. An engine was leaving the goods yard towards the main line to work the 11.25 a.m. train to the junction. It somehow managed to run into the stop block against the west signal box, moving it completely. The engine was derailed and the line was torn up. A guard's brake van was also badly damaged. Fortunately, the main line was still in working order and traffic was not held up, except that the 11.25 a.m. could not be run. By the afternoon, a breakdown gang had sorted out the incident.

This photograph shows Mr Harry Shadbolt receiving a long service medal from the then stationmaster, Mr W. Chamberlayne. Harry started work at the Great Western Railway in 1915, but was called for active service in the First World War.

Emergency evacuation timetable from Acton & Ealing Broadway 1939

The timetable for the transportation of the evacuees from London. Chipping Norton is highlighted.

Above, below and previous page: The evacuees arriving at Chipping Norton station.

He enlisted in the Army and joined the Royal Warwickshire Regiment as Private 306579. He saw action in France, Belgium, Germany and Italy, and thankfully survived uninjured to be awarded the British War and Victory medals. After the war ended, Harry returned to the railway in Chipping Norton and then became a porter at the stations in Moreton-in-Marsh, Stretton-on-Fosse and Shipston-on-Stour. He later became a goods guard on the Honeybourne to Moreton-in-Marsh line. He retired from the railway on 24 February 1962 after forty-seven years' service. When he was interviewed by the *Banbury Guardian*, he advised youngsters not to join the railway as, in his opinion, there was no future in it. He said after forty-seven years' service, his wages were £10 10s per week. He remembered the many excursion trains that ran through every day, including the Newcastle to Swansea express that would take passengers to the seaside and beyond, which were already being cut back in his day. His comments proved interesting as only four years after his retirement, Dr Beeching closed many lines and stations.

Harry Shadbolt receiving his award.

Above and below: The train crashed into the west signal box.

Harry Shadbolt as a young man on Chipping Norton station.

Mr Shadbolt also remembered the agricultural show that was held at Chipping Norton. It brought in crowds from all over the country by train. Shown in the photograph with Mr Chamberlayne and Mr Shadbolt are Monty Harding, Phillip Pantin and John Langham.

During the period 1923–29 there was a drop in passenger numbers from 30,455 to 9,951, but the parcels and delivery increased slightly over the same period. The fall in passenger numbers was due to the transfer of railway road transport services to the local bus company.

In 1948, Chipping Norton station became a centre for the Zonal Delivery Scheme, the goods shed being modified with a series of loading bays constructed. This enabled goods to be unloaded from wagons into the waiting lorries for local delivery.

In the Reshaping of British Railways report it was decided to close the Kingham to Chipping Norton line and the last passenger train ran on 1 December 1962. The youngest passenger on this last train was twenty-two-month-old Joanna Richards. Her mother, Joan, of Albion Place, said, 'We travel everywhere by car nowadays and thought if we didn't take this chance, Joanna might never ride on a train locally again.' Schoolboys let off fireworks and Mr Ken Hughes, engine driver for eighteen years, said, 'Everybody seems to think it is a great joke, but I am not laughing!' Mrs Phyllis Carey of Station House, Kingham, whose late husband was a stationmaster at Kingham station, was on the train together with her pet dog Rex, daughter and son-in-law, Mr & Mrs E. C. Bond of Churchill. Most of the passengers were railway enthusiasts. Mrs T. Stanley of West End, Chipping Norton, took her thirteen-year-old son Patrick for the last journey. At Chipping Norton station, several handicapped children, under the watchful eye of superintendent W. S. Hughes from the National Children's Home, watched the train pull out, many of them not having seen a train before. Driver Ken Hughes gave two or three tugs on the whistle, but they sounded very plaintive in the fog. A bright, young girl asked her mother as they approached Sarsden Halt, 'Why aren't we going faster Mummy?' Her mother answered, 'It is a funeral dear, and you don't go fast at a funeral!'

Freight traffic finished on the line in 1964. The line was then dismantled and the land reverted to agricultural use.

Above and below: Inside the Chipping Norton goods shed.

A postcard to let relatives know the time and date of your departure or arrival.

Chipping Norton station with the goods shed in the background.

The well-maintained station garden at Chipping Norton.

A light Priory engine in the station.

Wallace the station cat with his catch of the day. Every self-respecting station had a cat and Chipping Norton was no exception. The railway cat's job was to keep rats and mice at bay, especially as perishable goods were carried on the lines. The only one of note at Chipping Norton was Wallace, a beautiful black-and-white tomcat who, if his photograph is anything to judge him by, thought a lot of himself and his prowess.

The 1926 general strike. The engine is being driven by Mr Norman Rowell, a local businessman, with fireman Bill Johnston and porter Fred Morse (who is obviously not on strike).

Engine *Fair Rosamund* in Chipping Norton station. Usually it was run on the Oxford to Worcester line. Wallace the cat is sat in prime position on the engine.

An AEC diesel car at Chipping Norton.

A noticeboard stating that the approach road to the station was a private road. The entrance gate was closed and locked every year on Good Friday.

The approach road to Chipping Norton station leading off Worcester Road.

Driver Ted Perry driving an auto train from Banbury to Kingham.

A view of the goods yard from the Bliss Mill.

The goods yard, taken from the common and showing the cattle dock, engine shed and the line of trees on the tramway.

A view of The Leys showing Chipping Norton coal wagons.

The Leys with five Bliss Mill wagons on the tracks.

W. S. Hitchman and his workmen having their photograph taken before going on a day's outing.

Above and below: A railway enthusiast excursion in Chipping Norton station.

Pupils from Chipping Norton Grammar School crossing over the bridge after returning from their holiday in Switzerland with their teachers, Mr and Mrs Ransome.

Chipping Norton station, 1960, showing the wartime building.

2

Railway Memories of Fred Warren
Grade I Porter 1932–45

On the last Friday of September 1939 two long trains arrived in Chipping Norton with teachers and the children from the New City Road school and mainly from the East End of London. Please take into account that other towns in the Cotswolds also had train loads. All went off very well because the teachers accompanying kept the children organised and the weather was fine.

However, we are told that there was a different feeling in the air on Saturday. The weather was wet and the trains carrying mothers and small children were scheduled to arrive from the East Ham area. When the fourteen coaches and vans arrived, they were overloaded. As the platform was too short for everyone to disembark simultaneously, the process took a long time and the photographer, Mr Packer, was able to take a lot of photographs.

The town saw many evacuees. They arrived at 3.30 p.m., as Fred Warren recalled. The Red Cross and St John's Ambulance were there to meet them and to provide water for the thirsty children. Each child was labelled and carried a gas mask and a suitcase. From the station they were taken by bus, or on foot, to the town, where they were sorted out in the Baptist schoolroom. From here they were taken to New Street Cinema, which was used for their reception area. There were 321 children and forty adults for Chipping Norton. A further 900 were billeted on the district after their reception at the town hall.

Furious rain came down and my Headquarters were clamouring for the empty train to be returned to Kingham and I firmly refused to disembark the second batch until there were signs of transport vehicles returning. Out small station shelters were already overcrowded unbearably ... no tents to protect them from the elements. We muddled through in good old British fashion.

As Mr Warren says, the branch line was a lifeline.

The railway also saw troop movement. The 50th Division Territorials, the Durhams, arrived and dispersed into neighbouring villages. They left at the end of January 1940; it was a cold, snowy day and vital railway equipment had to be defrosted before there could be any movement.

On Saturday 1 June 1940, the stationmaster recalled that two guards' regiments were booked to 'detrain', as he said, at Chipping Norton. According to him, they had come direct from Dunkirk, without equipment and with some who were slightly wounded. These received first aid treatment. Residents in New Street and nearby streets were awoken to find the Durham soldiers resting in their front gardens, cold, hungry and totally exhausted. Many cups of tea and toast were readily given out to these very brave men.

The railway was hit by some incendiary bombs, and there had been one bomb on the station premises, but nothing more.

A big event was the unloading of American munitions and distributing them on the side of the main roads around the town, ready to be picked up on D-Day. Chipping Norton became popular with the personnel involved when they discovered the availability of local beer

3

SARSDEN SIDINGS & HALT

The early construction was known as Sarsden Sidings because, although near Churchill village, the name of Churchill was already on the Great Western Railway map – to avoid confusion the name Sarsden was used. Others would consider that the name was used to honour James Langston MP, who, as the owner of Sarsden House, had enabled the building of the railway. You can take your pick.

Sarsden Halt is situated 2½ miles from the hamlet of Sarsden. It was situated at the bottom of a lane leading to the mill, with the remains of the original medieval village close by. The lane crossed the railway and wound its way through the mill yard.

Sarsden Siding was equipped with a signal box. Goods and passengers were transported from the sidings. It is known that a man was prosecuted for travelling without a ticket from here, even though there was no ticket office at the time. In 1912, there was a similar occurrence when a man again was prosecuted for non-payment of fare. However, he was known for having committed this offence previously.

Thomas Lee was the gatekeeper, porter, signalman, ticket collector and salesman at the sidings in the 1890s. He died in Chipping Norton and was buried at Churchill on 4 January 1913. He had ten children. Thomas would have found himself in charge of a halt and not just sidings once the platform had been added in 1906.

The photograph on page 76 shows the unloading of coal onto horse-drawn wagons to take up into the village. The wagon belonged to William Peachey, who was the publican at The Chequers in Churchill. The coal usually came from the Griff Colliery, Coton Chivers, Nuneaton, but sometimes it was from the Coventry coal mines. The tracks for the branch lines would have been recycled main line tracks. The building in the background is Churchill Mill.

Also to be seen are the wooden slats of the steps leading to the wooden platform. Some of the wood used was from recycled sleepers.

Another railway employee at Sarsden Halt was Arthur Bunting. He later moved to become signalman at Bruern Crossing on the main Oxford to Worcester line.

The halt viewed through the level crossing.

The halt looking from the goods yard.

A timetable board, which can now be seen at Winchcombe Railway Museum.

The signal box with Thomas Lee in the centre.

Unloading coal at the halt.

Above and below: General views of the halt.

Sarsden Halt in May 1961.

The former side of Sarsden Halt in March 2014.

4

CHURCHILL CROSSING

This part of the line was known initially as Kingham Crossing because it was at the point where the Churchill–Kingham road crossed it and ran parallel to Mill Lane, the road leading to Sarsden Halt. It was put in when the railway was first constructed in 1855, and Sarsden and Churchill were the only manned level crossings within sight of each other on the Banbury–Cheltenham line. When it was first built it was known as Kingham Crossing. William Dickens was the first known crossing keeper. The memorial on his grave at Churchill cemetery states, 'For thirty-eight years a railway official at the Kingham Crossing.'

He was born in Bledington in 1813 and married Anne Walker from Moreton-in-Marsh. They had seven children, the last three being born at Churchill. The tiny crossing cottage must have been terribly crowded. One son, John, was stationmaster at Fladbury in 1873, and then stationmaster at Eynsham in 1881.

In 1883, the *Banbury Guardian* reported:

The man in charge of the crossing between Churchill and Kingham saw a dog straying up the line – called for it to go off – it took no notice ... the man (who has lost both his hands) held up his arm to drive the animal away ... it seized him by the legs ... poor fellow's wife came with a flagstaff ... it loosed his grip ... ran in the direction of Kingham. The dog also bit a child at Foscote ... and the miller's child at Bledington ... a child called Stayte ... and a female servant. It was foaming at the mouth and tearing up grass ... it was shot by Mr Bolter, Junior – killed by the blacksmith with a hammer.

Thanks to Ralph Mann for this story!

The Chipping Norton Deanery had a delightful obituary to William Dickens.

William died at his son-in-law's house at Chipping Norton on February 10th 1895. His well-known figure will be missed by all, strangers as well as friends, who were accustomed to see him walking on the Churchill Road. In spite of the accident which deprived him of both arms, when comparatively young, he had a singularly happy expression. For many years his post was to attend to the railway gates on the road to Kingham.

Note the variation in the description of his disability!

Thomas Wilkins Leadbetter was the second crossing keeper. He arrived from Fairford in 1894 and stayed until his death in 1906. During his time, Kingham Crossing was renamed Churchill Crossing. The order for the new nameboard was put in on 18 July 1899.

Arthur George Watkins was born at Aston, near Bampton, in 1878 and worked on the GWR. While working at Paddington goods yard he met his future wife, Alice Gertrude Eamer, whose father was an inspector at Paddington. During his time there he lost a leg in an accident when a wagon broke loose and ran over the leg. No compensation was paid, but he was given another occupation on the railways as a gatekeeper at Churchill Crossing. His wage was 6s per week. A cottage went with the job. It was extremely small but had two bedrooms. They had six children, but three boys slept at Arthur's mother's house in Kingham Road, Churchill. He was keeper for twenty-eight years. As Mr Watkins had lost a leg, he had a few problems with mobility. When groceries were needed he used to hand his shopping basket and money to the fireman on the train. This fireman then took it to Chipping Norton station where the stationmaster promptly sent a porter to do the shopping. It was then sent back to Churchill Crossing on the next train. Rumour has it that he never wore a hat and he wore his railway cap only when the Port to Port (Newcastle to Swansea) Express came through.

The Churchill Crossing cottage, *c.* 1908, with Arthur Watkins, his wife and daughter, Nancy.

Right: Arthur Watkins standing by the signal control leavers.

Below: Jim Watkins watching the Down Port to Port on its way to Swansea. The Port to Port Express was hauled by a 4300 class locomotive, which would have taken over the train at Banbury.

Sometime in May in the 1920s, a fully loaded dray from Hitchman's brewery was going to Stow Fair when it was struck by a light engine travelling from Kingham. The engine was, in fact, making an unauthorised journey along the line and so should not have been there. The drayman was unhurt but the dray was destroyed and Mr Watkins said, 'Marbles were sent everywhere from all the lemonade bottles. We buried them at the roads.'

A lovely story relating to Arthur Watkins is passed around his family. Mrs Watkins was in her kitchen clearing up after her husband's funeral, as she was expected to leave the railway premises almost immediately. A knock came at the door and there was a railway porter bearing a cardboard box. 'This came from Paddington, Missus.' Mrs Watkins, somewhat puzzled, took the box, thanked the man and turned back into the cottage. 'Wonder what they've sent me,' she said, untying the string. Lifting the lid she was astonished to find that the box was empty. However, at the bottom was a piece of paper. Unfolding it, she read, 'Instructions to return wooden leg. Kindly put in box and return to Paddington.'

'Well I never!' she exploded. 'The cheek! I'll tell 'em.'

The crossing cottage in the early 1930s. Note that the cottage has hanging tiles.

Arthur Bunting, Arthur ? and Arthur Watkins, all GWR employees. Each man had an artificial leg and they are pictured engaged in a game of yo-yos.

William Cook was the last keeper at the crossing.

Furious and red in the face, she wrote a note to the railways officials and sent it along with the box by the next train to Paddington. A clerk at the main line station opened it and read, 'If you want Mr Watkins' wooden leg, come and get it! Bring a spade 'cos I buried him and it yesterday!'

The last keeper of the crossing was William Cook. He worked from about 1946 until the closure of the railway in 1964. He moved with his daughter, Beryl, to live in a council house in Churchill.

A sad day in May 1966 when the track was lifted.

5

CHIPPING NORTON JUNCTION

In 1853, there was no station between Adlestrop and Shipton-under-Wychwood, and so, on 10 August 1855, a branch line to Chipping Norton was inaugurated by the Chipping Norton Railway. It was named Chipping Norton Junction even though it was in Churchill parish. In 1882, a section of the Banbury & Cheltenham Direct Railway was opened. It connected Bourton-on-the-Water to the OW&WR at Chipping Norton Junction. The first known buildings were erected in the same style as the Bourton-on-the-Water railway, which opened on 1 March 1862.

The GWR rebuilt the station to their style in the 1880s. The brick was yellow and blue, overhanging with awnings like a valance, as you can see in the picture. The woodwork was painted in their colours of light and dark stone.

The shelter on the central platform of Chipping Norton Junction was built by the GWR in their style. As it was originally laid with broad gauge as well as standard gauge – making it a mixed gauge track – there was a greater width between the platforms, which can be seen in the photograph.

For nearly twenty years any through trains running between Banbury and Cheltenham Spa St James needed to reverse at the Chipping Norton Junction. This was found to be inconvenient for trains that did not need to call at the Junction.

In 1906, a flyover, known as the loop, was erected over the Oxford to Worcester line to connect the Chipping Norton branch to the Bourton-on-the-Water line. Trains for Cheltenham could travel straight over without having to shunt in the station.

With the building of the loop, two new signal boxes were added to the two already in place. Unusually, they were named after the four points of the compass. The main line boxes were north and south, whereas the loop boxes were called east and west. In 1922, the south box became redundant and the north box was renamed Kingham Station Signal Box.

Chipping Norton Junction, *c.* 1875. The stationmaster was Aden Eaton.

The first station at Bourton-on-the-Water.

The loop being built.

The south signal box.

CHIPPING NORTON JUNCTION.

Above, below and next page: General views of Chipping Norton Junction.

CHIPPINGNORTON JUNCTION.

Note that the signal box is tall because it was built up against the road bridge and the signalman needed to see over the bridge. To avoid a confusion of names, the station was renamed Kingham in May 1909.

Kingham station had a considerable number of staff, including the stationmaster, porters, shunters, clerks and ticket collectors. People who worked on the rail track were known as the Permanent Way staff. They had an inspector at Kingham who was responsible for the Chipping Norton, Hook Norton, Charlbury, Shipton-under-Wychwood areas. Each small area worked under a ganger over whom the inspector had charge.

Kingham station staff. From left to right, back row: shunter Hector Townsend, porter Ernest Worrell, porter Charlie Hall, porter Bob Jakeman, porter Horace Matthews, shunter Hedley Frankling. Front row: -?-, Miss Andrews, station foreman Horace Markham, clerk Cyril Stayt.

Permanent Way staff: George Slatter, Lewis Hall, John Stayt, Charlie Franklin, -?-, Jack Collett, George Winter, Fred Hill, Dick Warren, John Warren, and ganger Leonard Hands.

Below are some of the names and dates we have of the Chipping Norton Junction and Kingham stationmasters.

Chipping Norton Junction
?–1858	William Hughes
1858–71	Edward Jackson Cuff
1871–79	Aden Eaton
1879–1906	John George Brecknell
1906–17	Charles Thomas Widdows

Kingham station
1917–26	William Insall
1926–?	George Farmer
?–?	Mr Curnock
1949	Oliver Henry Carey
1948–66	T. W. H. Lane

William Insall was born in Chipping Norton and was the son of the Mr and Mrs John Insall of New Street. He had been in the Great Western Railway's service for forty-five years, entering as a clerk aged eighteen. He was chief goods clerk at Evesham for many years before being appointed stationmaster at Wenlock. He then served at Colwell before becoming stationmaster at Kingham, where he served for eight years before his retirement.

George Farmer was the stationmaster who, about one month after his appointment, was caught up in the general strike. He was interested in union affairs and was vice president of the North Oxfordshire Divisional Labour Party. It is surprising, therefore, that he did not encourage one of his porters to go on strike, but had he done so the porter might have lost his job and George did not want him to suffer this. We can assume from George's son's account that, as the porter had asked about his going on strike while he was on railway land, George, despite his union beliefs, upheld GWR regulations. However, he himself went on strike and, as a result, did not return either to Kingham or to the position of stationmaster, but was given a more lowly job as a fifth-grade clerk at Pershore, dealing with plum traffic. He was working under a man he had trained twenty years before (not a plum job, one would say).

Stationmaster Mr Curnock was buried at Churchill on 15 June 1953, aged sixty-three. Oliver Carey retired due to ill health, but stayed on in the stationmaster's house. Stationmaster T. W. H. Lane, also known as Bert, lived in Chipping Norton, which is why Oliver Carey could retain the stationmaster's house. Bert had been a clerk at Chipping Norton station and worked there for forty-five years altogether. He retired as area manager at Oxford. He was the last stationmaster to be employed at Kingham. There was no further classification of the post.

A 3200 class engine outside the engine shed with a view of the yard.

Above, below and next page: General views of Kingham station after 1909.

The water tower, engine shed and station signal box.

Flooding in Bledington Road near to the station with Tom Rose and his dog.

Children collecting for the Belgian refugees on Kingham station.

Kingham station staff with stationmaster William Ansell on the central platform.

Staff at Kingham station.

Wintry scene at Kingham.

Above and below: The last passenger auto train with engine No. 4507 from Banbury to Kingham station on 2 June 1951. The driver was B. Townsend with fireman D. Baker from Banbury locomotive shed. It was decorated with the Union Jack and a laurel leaf.

GWR boundary marker, dated 1900, which was positioned on the road bridge into Kingham.

Single line working token used from Kingham station to Chipping Norton and vice versa.

Kingham station before 1962 with the branch train on the left and the main train line on the right.

A stalled engine at Kingham sidings.

6

THE LANGSTON ARMS HOTEL

Adjoining the railway premises was the Langston Arms Hotel. It was built in 1879 by Henry Reynolds-Moreton, 3rd Earl of Ducie. This was originally built as a hunting lodge with stabling for several horses. Stone was used from a local quarry previously owned by the Earl of Ducie's father-in-law, Squire Langston. George Devey, a highly respected architect, was employed to design and carry out the project. The Langston Arms was later used for guests, mainly travelling on the local railway.

Kelly's Directory for 1883 lists Mark Prior as the proprietor of the hotel. By 1891, the proprietor was Walter Henry Hawker, followed by his son George in 1921.

The Langston Arms at Kingham station.

George Hawker.

The hotel was leased to the Stroud Brewery Co. Ltd for twenty-one years from 29 September 1907, the rent being £140 per annum. Stroud Brewery purchased the hotel at the Sarsden Estate sale in 1922. They paid £4,400 for it. In 1897, an agreement was reached with the hotel and GWR that the footbridge from the station to the hotel could still be used, but the passengers at Kingham station could use the footbridge to go to and from the hotel only when they were changing trains at the station. A porter would be sent to the hotel to tell passengers when the train was arriving.

In 1985, it was sold again. It is now a respected home for patients with dementia problems, as well as providing nursing facilities for elderly people with mobility and physical disabilities.

When the annual Cheltenham Races were held in March, the Royal Train could often be seen overnight in the sidings. The young children of Bledington often walked over the fields to look at this train and were usually lucky to glimpse the King and Queen and the two Princesses, who would sometimes wave and acknowledge them.

Adjacent to the Langston Arms Hotel was the Kingham stockyard, where sales of livestock were regularly held. In 1914, the auctioneers were Paxton & Holiday. Later it was run by Tayler, Fletcher & Villar, who were auctioneers in Cold Aston, Cheltenham. Specialist sales of shorthorn cattle were held there. Cattle were sold to customers from around the world. They were then despatched in special wagons known as beetle prize cattle wagons.

Lainchbury's was a firm of agricultural engineers in the village of Kingham. In the 1920s, they bought patents for an elevator from Robinsons of Deanshanger. They modified the plans and made a lighter model under their own name, which they called 'superlite'. These were sent by train to destinations all over the world.

Kingham was one of the regular venues where pigeons were released. In this photograph, taken before the Second World War, 15,000 pigeons are being released, mostly from the North of England. Local people often wondered whether they all found their way home. When the railway stopped transporting livestock, pigeons were brought to Kingham by specialist lorries, from which they were then released.

A pedigree shorthorn cattle auction. Buyers are standing on a harvest wagon.

Thomas Sollis leading one of the shorthorn cows to be loaded on to the train.

RAILWAY STATION:
CHIPPING NORTON JUNCTION

SARSDEN ESTATE OFFICE
CHIPPING NORTON
OXON

TELEGRAPH: CHURCHILL OXON

27th Novr. 1907

Dear Sirs. C. N. Junction Sale Yard

I have now received a tender from Messrs Bayliss Jones & Bayliss for the proposed iron fencing as per plan submitted to you on the 18th inst. & which amounts to £287 or with stronger pillars £304. – This does not include any haulage or concrete required to fix the standards. –

I have written as above to Mr Tayler. –

I remain

Yours faithfully

Jos. M. Blair

Messrs Holiday & Son
Auctioneers
Bicester

Right: Letter to Mr Holiday at Bicester about the price of fencing for the building of cattle pens.

Below: Renovating of the saleyards.

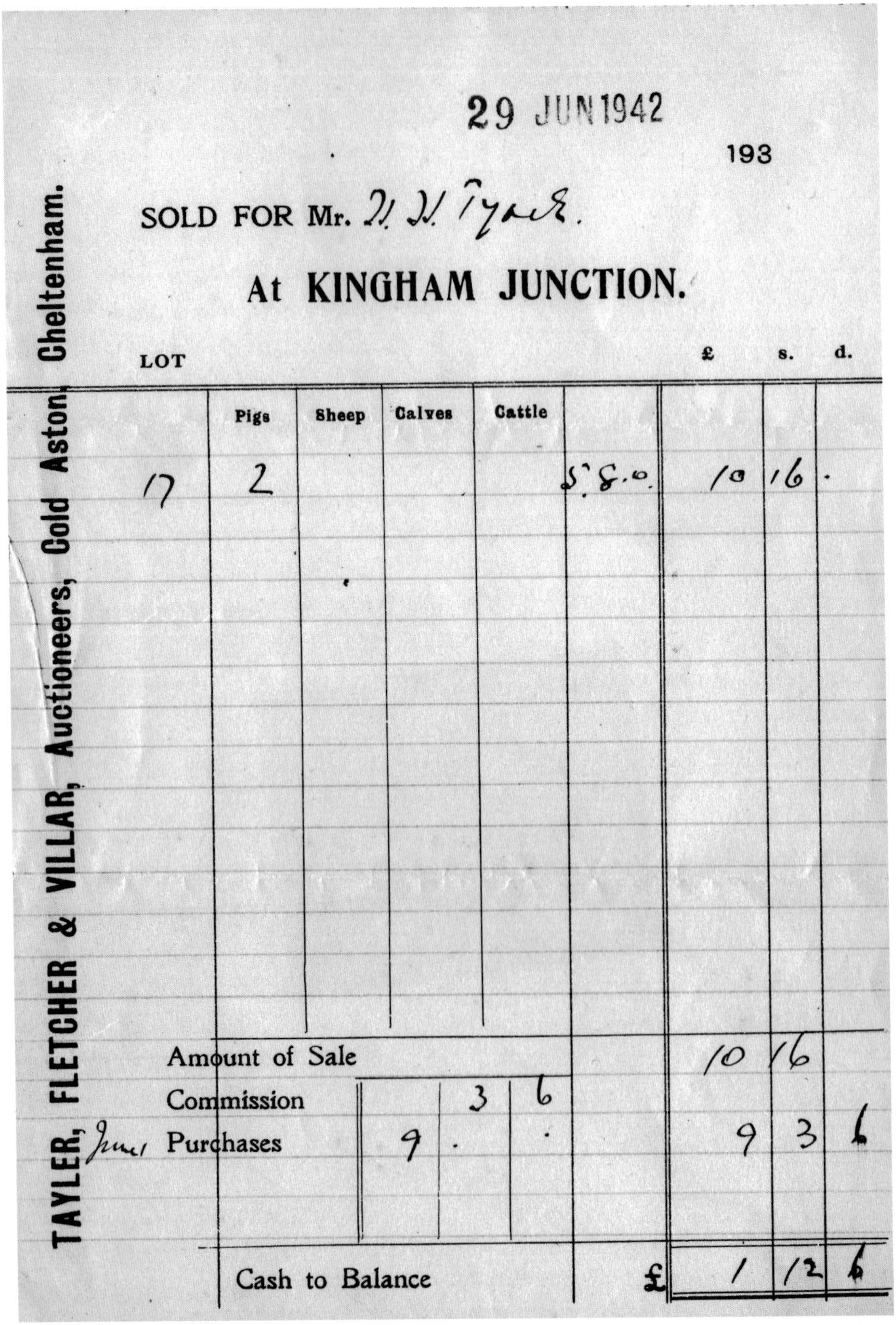

29 JUN 1942

193

SOLD FOR Mr. *N. N. Tyack.*

At KINGHAM JUNCTION.

LOT	Pigs	Sheep	Calves	Cattle		£	s.	d.
17	2				5.8.0	10	16	·
Amount of Sale						10	16	
Commission			3	6				
Jun Purchases	9	·	·			9	3	6
Cash to Balance					£	1	12	6

TAYLER, FLETCHER & VILLAR, Auctioneers, Cold Aston, Cheltenham.

Sales receipt from 1942 for two pigs.

Above and below: Lainchbury & Sons elevators loading on the trains.

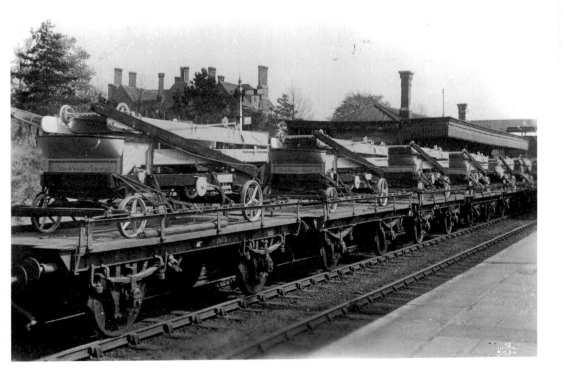

Pigeons in baskets before release.

Releasing pigeons at Kingham station.

7

KINGHAM STATION CRASH

On 15 July 1966, fourteen people were injured in a rail crash at Kingham station when the rear coach of a Hereford–Paddington express derailed. This was the first accident of any consequence of a passenger train on the Kingham line for a long time. A gang of men working on the line were fortunately having their lunch at the time – a lucky escape. The track was buckled and torn up near the station signal box. The rear coach came off the track at a disused set of points and broke free of the rest of the train. It struck the southbound platform and flipped onto its side. When it finally came to rest, it was against the opposite platform, near to a large station signboard.

Fourteen people were injured, four of them seriously. The only member of staff on duty at that time was porter H. W. Hemmings, who was making a cup of tea when he heard the bang of the express. 'I saw the rear coach was off the track and was showing up sparks and scattering ballast.' One of the first on the scene was Joe Ahern, who was the proprietor of the station garage. Mrs Aherne telephoned for help while Mr Ahern and Michael Wellstood took ladders to help passengers escape from the damaged coach. Mr J. K. Forty, who was a ticket inspector from Worcester, was on the coach at the time. 'I felt a series of bumps and was thrown on my back. I was thrown along the length of the corridor and received cuts and bruises.' Eight ambulances were called and took casualties to Chipping Norton Hospital and the Radcliffe Infirmary in Oxford. The Chipping Norton Fire Brigade was also in attendance. The express train was allowed to resume its journey to Paddington after a forty-five minute delay. Repairs to the track were completed in two days.

The public enquiry into the crash, which was held eleven days later, came to the conclusion that it was caused by some locking nuts missing from the points, which allowed the switch rail to move.

Above and below: A rail accident – the last carriage is seen off the rails, leaning against the platform.

8

KINGHAM RAILWAY WORKERS

There are many sources relating to the railway men of Kingham, and these have been used by the Revd Ralph Mann to give us a glimpse into their backgrounds and lives.

The advent of the railway branch line from Chipping Norton to Kingham brought a welcome change in the lives of the local people, not least in their work. Farm work was, of course, seasonal, and wages were not always regular. The railway provided opportunities for regular work and payment and for the possibility of promotion, although the agricultural labourer would not appear to advance beyond the role of railway worker. However, we learn from the census returns that Charles Pearse, described as an agricultural labourer in 1851, and specifically as a shepherd in 1861, started work on the railway as a labourer, but was a platelayer by 1891.

Similarly, Shadrach Bridge, one of a number of that family who found work at Kingham, is described as a gardener's labourer in 1881, but ten years later he, too, is a platelayer.

Inevitably, sons followed their fathers into work. Of the eighty-seven families listed, the families of Adams, Collett, Slade and Smith, had both father and son working for the railway, as did cousins and nephews of the Bridge family. On the whole, their work was that of pointsman, porter or platelayer. It was possible to achieve a higher status in the last two jobs to become foremen. Both Kendrick Beck and Leonard Harries rose to be platelayer foremen, and Alfred Gomm and George Grafton became porter foremen, the latter also being described as a goods foreman.

There was enough variety of work for people of different skills and abilities to find employment in and around the station. As well as the work already mentioned, there were the following jobs: inspector (including permanent way inspector), signalman, booking clerk, carriage maker, and ganger or, as he could be called, line superintendent.

On 26 December 1921, a GWR memorandum was sent to T. Bolter, permanent way inspector at Kingham, relating to rules that he had to read out to those who

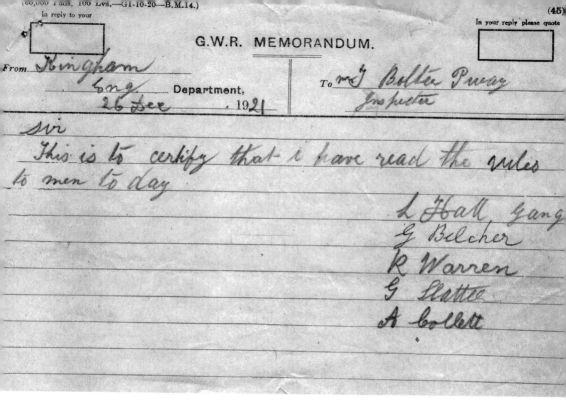

(00,000 Tads, 100 Lvs.—G1-10-20—B.M.14.)

In reply to your

G.W.R. MEMORANDUM.

In your reply please quote

From Kingham

Eng Department,

26 Dec .192 1

To mr J Bolter Pwway

Inspector

Sir

This is to certify that i have read the rules to men to day

L Hall gang
G Belcher
R Warren
G Slatter
A Collett

GWR memorandum.

were involved, in this case his gang. Listing the names of the gang he had to indicate that he had fulfilled the task. As we have a copy of one of the many memoranda sent out, it was obviously filed at the station. Rules might relate to trespass and encroachment upon land, for example.

A man could also work as a yardman, crossing gate opener (perhaps later described as crossing gate keeper), engine driver – a post that became every little boy's dream – and, most important of all, the stationmaster. There were other posts available: telegraph repairer or engineer brakesman, junior guard, engine cleaner, packer on the line and stoker. Most probably there were other jobs not included, as indeed there must have been many more employees not mentioned because they were not around at the time of the census and, like the seasons, they came, produced what was asked of them, and flitted off elsewhere. The navvy would have been one of these. Seeking work wherever the railway companies needed people to prepare the land for a new line, they came from as far away as Wisbech in Norfolk. Once the work was done, a navvy would leave the area to try his luck elsewhere, unless he married.

William Porter was one of these. From West Walton, near Wisbech, he is described as having carpentry skills. Once in Kingham working as a navvy, he married Lucy Bridge and settled down as a carpenter, carrier and odd-job man. He died aged seventy-one years, but one can imagine that he had a satisfactory life.

Benoni Walker, also from Norfolk, rose from navvy to superintendent. He, too, married but nothing else is known of him in the area after the 1851 census.

William Porter met his wife because he lodged with her family. The area would see an influx of newcomers, especially at the time of construction. A large number of workers would be from Kingham and the neighbouring villages, but there were many others from neighbouring counties: Shropshire, Gloucestershire and Worcestershire in particular. Many of these would have required lodgings as they had moved solely to get work, not necessarily to settle down. If a person was widowed or had a spare room then there was a chance of making a little extra money by having a lodger. Some of the 'landlords' included John Belcher, Robert Brick and Elizabeth Hemmings – whose age is given as eighteen – Thomas Bridges and, as already noted, William and Elizabeth Bridge, whose daughter married William Porter. Marriages took place within the railway community. William Betteridge, the son of engine driver Richard, married Hannah Maria Slade, the daughter of William, a porter, signalman and switchman. Thomas Brecknell's wife was Beatrice Mary Eaton, the daughter of Aden, who, like himself, was an engine driver. Similarly, the daughter of Thomas Bridge, described as a railway labourer, married Thomas Adams, a railway pointsman.

As well as providing work, the railway also caused accidents. A young lad of twelve named Thomas William Bye, a railway clerk even at that tender age, was run over by a locomotive at Churchill and subsequently died of his injuries. As we have already seen, Arthur George Watkins lost his leg while working on the railway, but this was at Paddington station. There must have been many more injuries and deaths than there are records of them, especially among the navvies. One of these, Noah Dore, who was only sixteen years old, died of a fractured skull, but we can only imagine the accident that caused it. 'One of the best men I ever knew' was a tribute to George Grafton of Bledington who 'met with a fatal accident at Chipping Norton Junction, November 9th 1895, aged 36 years'. The gravestone continues:

Our friend has gone before
To that celestial shore
He hath left his mates behind
He hath all the storms outrode
Found the rest we fail to find
Landed in the arms of God

Charles Seabury Nairn was another victim of a steam engine from which he fell. He was then run over by a train.

The seven Hall brothers worked on the railway in the 1950s: John, Charles, Frederick, Walter, Cecil, Arthur and Harold.

A Curiosity

We know of one famous person who specified in his will that on his death he was to be brought by train to the Junction (Kingham station) for his burial at Idbury. Sir Benjamin Baker (1840–1907) was well known for his design of the Forth Bridge. He was also the architect and engineer of the first Aswan Dam. In his will he requested that twelve black ponies be harnessed to his hearse to pull the coffin up the long hill from the Junction to Idbury churchyard. The cortege consisted of many notable people who had come by the special train from London.

9

KINGHAM & METHODISM

The Revd Mann draws our attention to the fact that 'the railways were influenced in spreading and strengthening nonconformity'. In 1851, Kingham chapel was founded and, in 1878, it was transferred to the Wesleyan Methodists. He suggests that ministers might travel on a circuit by train and that in this area Kingham would be the centre.

As has already been written, the job of stationmaster was recognisably superior to that of other work in the village. John George Brecknell was stationmaster at Chipping Norton Junction by the 1881 census records of Churchill. He had taken on the position in 1879, and retired on 14 April 1906. He took an active part in village affairs, being chairman of the parish meeting anf overseer from 1908–14, during which time he was school manager and manager of the village green. He lived at Eardington Cottage and was considered gentry.

George Adams became a churchwarden in 1893 and remained so until 1901, during which time he was a parish councillor. From 1899–1908 he was an overseer of the poor. It is known that he was also a draper and grocer in Kingham in 1895. Perhaps one can conclude that, having retired from the railway and taken a more obvious community post in the village, he became more interested in, and involved with, community affairs.

Several men with less prestigious jobs also became involved in church and village affairs. Shadrach Bridge has no record of rail work after 1891, when he was forty-one years old, but from 1890–1908 he was a trustee of Kingham Wesleyan chapel, as was James Bulloch in the same period. James was then reappointed and, in 1903, was chapel steward and secretary, and then superintendent of the Wesleyan Sunday school. In 1908, he resigned his offices at the chapel because of ill health but was reappointed chapel steward in 1908. He died in 1912.

Albert Cottrell, a signalmen, acted as a parish councillor for a year, but as there are no references to him after this, one can only conclude that he left the area.

Another stationmaster of note in this community was Aden Eaton. It is recorded that he was stationmaster at Chipping Norton Junction until 1879. From 1881 at least he also devoted his time to community affairs. He was a grocer, draper

Tomb of Sir Benjamin Baker in Idbury churchyard.

The Forth Bridge.

Stationmaster John Brecknell and his family, taken outside the stationmaster's house in 1885. From left to right, back row: Thomas, Walter, Annie, Charles, Rhosa, Jack, Alice and George. Front row: John George Brecknell, Albert and Rhoda. Daughter Emily is not in the photograph.

and baker, and so very much involved in the village life. Twice he became overseer of the poor for a total of four years. Adding postmaster and agent for wines and spirits to his job as a grocer, he returned to the church as churchwarden in 1896. From 1894, he was a parish councillor for five years, becoming vice chairman of the council. On 9 September 1872, he was made a foundation trustee of Kingham Wesleyan chapel until 1890. He was both steward and treasurer. Revd Mann concludes, 'he must have been elected people's churchwarden in 1896, in order to qualify for dual membership of the two churches.'

Leonard James Hands showed leadership qualities through his activities. He was a ganger and a line superintendent, indicating an ability to direct men and an interest in so doing. He was about forty-six when he was first mentioned in connection with the Wesleyan chapel. As a ganger, he became a trustee of the chapel in 1908, and remained a secretary and treasurer until 15 February 1937. He was obviously very trusted. He was a Sunday school teacher from 1889 'and succeeded James Bulloch as superintendent in 1912'. Very much involved in village affairs, he was elected a parish councillor, became a trustee of the green, overseer for two years and school manager for four years until 1914. He was also a trustee of Fuel Allotments in 1913. He applied to the charity commissioners to set up

Charity Trustees in the village, and was appointed one of the first trustees. He was responsible for the dedication of the lychgate in memory of Revd Lockwood. Mr Hands seemed to have made himself a prominent figure in Kingham. Born in 1853, he died in Kingham in 1937.

Others who were trustees of the Wesleyan chapel, chapel stewards or overseers were foreman George Grafton, William Slade and platelayer John James Stayt. The stationmaster at Kingham Junction, Charles F. Thomas Widdows, was made a trustee of Kingham Wesleyan chapel and chapel steward. How long he retained these offices is not recorded but he also died in 1937 in Swindon, aged ninety-one.

Kingham was important. From a small village it developed into an important junction on the branch line. Its position on the railway network encouraged a wider variety of work and an influx of people from both nearby and further afield. Comings and goings must have seemed part of village life and assumed their own importance. Village life developed. Today, Kingham is still an important place. It is a village but there is a wide diversity of work and activity. The station is still important as it connects with the capital and comings and goings reflect a continuous movement between the Cotswolds and London.

10

THE END OF THE LINE

Chipping Norton station finally closed for passengers on Saturday 1 December 1962.

> Steam symbol of an age which
> Benefits to be lasting and which lay,
> Through the counties...
> A regular solid permanent way.
>
> Join now the legendary charms,
> Recalled by place or by tavern sign.
> Soon will the Station Road or The Platelayers' Arms
> Be the last record of the valley line.

John Pudney, *Valediction for a Branch Railway*

> Chipping Norton chariot-
> Chippy Dick we called you –
> Contented little tank engine,
> Cherub cheeks blown out,
> Daily roughing it in cuttings as you
> Carried Chippy's pride,
> Where are you now?

Alan Gibbs, *Oxfordshire Memories*

So does anything of this line survive? Kingham station did not close, instead it developed into a thriving rail centre on the Worcester to London line. Daily it carries many commuters into Oxford and beyond.

Children from the National Children's Home watching the last passenger train from Chipping Norton to Kingham leave the station.

Chipping Norton station during demolition with Worcester road bridge in the background.

The old stable block before it was renovated. It is now a listed building.

The last remaining GWR building, which was the old stable block.

Above and below: The new station building at Kingham built in the 1990s by Arthur Groves & Sons.

The Up platform shelter today.

General view looking towards station buildings in 2014.

Looking down on to the former Chipping Norton station, now a builders' merchant's yard, February 2014.

The 86¾ milestone from the Chipping Norton branch line.

The filling in of the branch line off the road bridge.

The bridge after it had been filled in.

A postcard of the day.

The Up platform nameboard on Kingham station with the 84¾ milestone to Paddington.

BIBLIOGRAPHY

Evans, R., *Refugees*

Jenkins, Stanley C., Bob Brown and Neil Parkhouse, *The Banbury and Cheltenham Direct Railway* (Lightmoor Press, 2004)

Mann, Revd R., *Kingham and Methodism*

Mann, Revd R., *Nineteenth Century Railwaymen* (1996)

Menary, Derek (compiler), *Chipping Norton and the Railway* (West Oxfordshire District Council)

Russell, James H., *The Banbury and Cheltenham Railway 1887–1962* (Oxford Publishing Company, 1977)

The Banbury Guardian

The Guardian

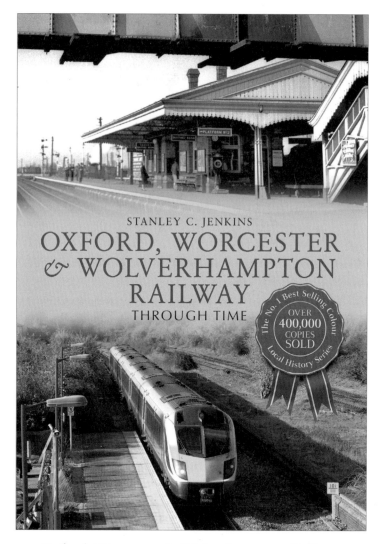

Oxford, Worcester & Wolverhampton Railway
Through Time

Stanley C. Jenkins

This fascinating selection of photographs traces some of the many
ways in which the Oxford, Worcester & Wolverhampton Railway
has changed and developed over the last century.

978 1 4456 1654 4
96 pages, full colour

Available from all good bookshops or order direct
from our website www.amberleybooks.com